Divorce

Divorce on a shoestring

DIY
Divorce

DIY
DIVORCE
Divorce on a shoestring

MICHELINE McCORMACK

MERLIN
PUBLISHING

Published in 2002 by
Merlin Publishing
16 Upper Pembroke Street
Dublin 2
Ireland
Tel: + 353 1 6764373
Fax: + 353 1 6764368
publishing@merlin.ie
www.merlin-publishing.com

British Library Cataloguing in Publication Data
A catalogue record for this book is available from
the British Library

ISBN 1–903582–21–0

5 4 3 2 1

Typeset by Carrigboy Typesetting Services
Cover design by Slick Fish Design
Printed by ColourBooks Ltd.

ACKNOWLEDGMENTS

One of the most interesting aspects of putting this book together was meeting and becoming acquainted with a group of new and stimulating people. And they all happen to be women.

I've often maintained that, having been in a career where I was surrounded by people at all times, there were really no surprises left to be discovered in any member of the human race. Of course, I hadn't met the team at Merlin then.

It's been a rewarding experience working with the dynamic duo, director and publisher Selga Medenieks and marketing and sales director Chenile Keogh. When they approached me about publishing this book, I warmed to their direct and upfront way which has never changed in all my dealings with them. That seems to be the approach of this team, as I discovered when I met their editorial manager Aoife Barrett and publicist Linda Kenny.

When you work with an editor like Roberta Reeners, it's easy to understand why every writer needs someone like her. She somehow manages to edit a manuscript without interfering with it or changing its structure. A rare gift, surely.

Since marriage break-down and divorce are now part of Irish life, there is a whole army of caring and efficient people involved in a network of organisations to cater for people affected by marital breakdowns. One such person in Prof. Ed McHale of the Clanwilliam Institute. Despite a heavy work load, he has always made himself available to me. I'm grateful for his contribution to this book.

Thanks are due also to Prof. Gabriel Kiely of the Family Study Group at UCD. His findings in his pilot study make interesting reading.

The team at Courts Services and the Family Mediation Service were always helpful and efficient. My thanks to them.

This book changed its shape, content and look on the way to completion, as most books do. But unfortunately, for legal reasons my interesting stories of celebrity divorces had to be omitted. But I appreciate the time that a number of well-known people gave me when telling me their stories.

James O'Toole and Jenny Muldoon were helpful too in times of Microsoft stress! As were Elizabeth and Vanessa O'Gorman and Niall McKenna.

Peter McIntyre deserves my thanks. And so too does my neighbour and friend, Charlotte O'Neill. I owe them.

There's a whole unknown team of designers and legal people at Merlin whom I may never meet — the back-room people who have helped put this book together. My appreciation goes to them.

I'm blessed, and have always been, in having good, worthwhile friends, both men and women. I mention them here because their interest and wholehearted support has been encouraging to me. All my friends are delightfully curious about this book but I suppose for me it's the feedback from my journalist pals which I've enjoyed just that bit more.

It's good to have the opportunity to be able to say publicly how much I care for and appreciate my family. I do, but they know that.

Finally, this book is really a book about courage — one woman's courage. Gay Gaynor is a rare kind of person, a strong-minded, intelligent woman whom I've been lucky enough to meet. I'm thankful that she has trusted me with the telling of her story.

MICHELINE MCCORMACK is a well-known journalist, broadcaster and author. As Woman's Editor for the Sunday World she wrote a popular, controversial column on social issues. She is the author of the bestselling book *Little Girl – The Lavinia Kerwick Story* and continues to contribute to many radio and television programmes nationwide. She lives in Dublin.

GAY GAYNOR, from Blanchardstown in Dublin, is a working mother with two teenage children. Now in her thirties, she is customer services representative at the Blanchardstown Shopping Centre, an appointment which she took up earlier this year. While studying and compiling her divorce papers, she was a secretary at the Blanchardstown Centre for the Unemployed.

Dr Ed McHale, BA, PhD, MFT, is managing director of the Clanwilliam Institute, Clanwilliam Terrace, Dublin, an organisation which provides personal, couple and family consultancy, organisational consultancy and professional training.

DEDICATION

To my friends
who have survived emotional break-ups
and who can still smile as they tell the tale.

CONTENTS

FOREWORD
Dr Ed McHale

Following two referenda, the first defeated and the second affirmed by a majority of less than 1%, divorce became legal in Ireland in 1997. It was predicted that divorce legislation would open the floodgates to marriage breakdowns with dire consequences, particularly to the women and children involved. This included such catastrophic outcomes as children being traumatised and emotionally impaired for life, with women abandoned and left impecunious and homeless.

Although it is apparent that such fears have not been realised, there are certainly individual stories of hardship and apparent injustice. Many have had to face the pain involved in ending an intimate relationship which they had hoped would last a lifetime. Ending such a relationship invariably involves loss — loss of companionship, loss of a partner to help manage the business of living and rearing a family, loss of what might have been, of the dream that was never attained.

Marriage breakdown and separation had occurred prior to 1997, of course, but the new legislation made remarriage possible. Second relationships, particularly those involving children, may be complex and challenging but they are now much more common. Indeed, the traditional nuclear family is just one of a wide range of household compositions. The possibility of remarriage now provides legal and social parameters for these second families, thus lessening the tendency to drift into and out of temporary relationships following separation.

The number of Irish households or family types which diverge from the traditional notion of two first-married parents and their children appears to be increasing at an accelerating rate. This, combined with the great variety of immigrants and refugees choosing to live here, is introducing enormous changes to Irish society. Our European neighbours have experienced these changes for a long time, so perhaps we have finally been drawn into the great momentum of these international trends.

How well will we cope with such change? I believe that the evidence to date is reassuring.

In spite of a natural resistance to change, we appear to have particular resources which enable us to reflect and discuss, to choose wise and informed ways of proceeding. Technological developments have also helped, particularly the media's ability to provide instant, dramatic reports of national and international events. Radio and television chat shows remain popular, and they provide the shop window for discussions about the complexity of contemporary life on this island.

I have been greatly impressed by my own first-hand experience of how couples now deal with marriage crises, especially as these affect their children. Couples appear to be less rigid, more willing to listen and to discuss the management of this potentially highly emotive subject. In general, women are now better prepared for the financial implications of independent living; and men are better informed about child-care and the difficulties of combining child-care and employment.

It sometimes comes as a surprise to separating couples that their children adjust to the situation more quickly than they do. Separation is not an easy process, and everyone involved will experience some degree of loss and sadness. But there need not be a long-term price. It is possible for all to adjust to the end of a marriage and to move on positively and productively. Children will do so if they are not caught in the middle and are not subjected to continued conflict between the parents. While parents must be able to express their own feelings of sadness and loss, they must also provide information which is appropriate to the children's level of understanding if they are to make sense of this confusing time. In my experience, families negotiating separation and divorce are now much more aware of this. And for those who are blinded by their own anxiety or loss and who fail to recognise the dangers of dividing their children's loyalties, a gentle reminder about the children's needs in these situations is usually sufficient for the parents to introduce more suitable practices.

A crisis by its very nature means that people are not prepared for it. However, couples in crisis now appear to have a better vocabulary for making sense of their emotional and personal confusion. Indeed a crisis may present the opportunity for introducing change through informed choice. It must not, however, be permitted to spin out of control, producing even greater confusion and more intractable conflict.

In a crisis, one partner may decide that the pain or the price of staying in the relationship is too great, that separating is the best option. The couple is then faced with the many challenges of achieving an independent, personal growth. While it is sometimes difficult for them to make sense of the situation in which they find themselves, there are more and more examples of people doing so successfully. While everyone getting married (apart from the extremely cynical) hopes for a lasting and fulfilling relationship, not every couple will achieve this. As there are good marriage and bad marriages, there are also good and bad separations. Neither bad marriages nor bad separations are in the best interest of the adults or children involved, or of society as a whole.

When the first independent professional counselling service for couples and families was established in 1982, the prevailing attitude was that marriage was for life, no matter what the cost. At the time, couples in chronic conflict often remained under the one roof. My previous work in child guidance clinics had brought me into contact with scores of children who had lived in such circumstances and whose suffering was both obvious and heart-rending. Although this was often apparent to their parents, acknowledging this suffering only served to increase their feelings of guilt and powerlessness, intensifying the pain and mutual torment in which the family members found themselves.

For the first time, this new counselling service, which became the Clanwilliam Institute, addressed the possibility that parting might be the most constructive option for the parents and the most beneficial arrangement for the children. It offered mediation, a professional service designed to help separating couples to draw up their own terms of separation and establish appropriate arrangements for the care of their children.

This new concept was completely at odds with the prevailing legal opinion which held that separating spouses were not capable of negotiating their own agreements and that the custody and physical care of the children were best entrusted to one parent, usually the mother. Quite quickly, however, many couples began to recognise the benefits of mediation and the possibility of succeeding in this very challenging process. They agreed to talk through their pain to achieve mutual agreement. The majority succeeded for many reasons, including a commitment to their children's welfare and the belief that they could manage their own lives successfully.

This book is the result of one woman's tenacity and determination. It is an acknowledgment of that inner spark of self, the recognition that it is possible to transcend an initial feeling of helplessness to achieve a purpose. It marks a realisation that we are capable of making profound decisions with a sense of responsibility, that we can overcome the most adverse and painful of circumstances.

While a picture may be worth a thousand words, an example of triumph against the odds is the ultimate inspiration.

FEW WINNERS

When film actress Jennifer Lopez paid $10 million to her husband of eight months, Chris Judd, for a divorce settlement, even the Hollywood cynics were shocked. No woman in Hollywood had ever paid out that kind of money to get a man out of her hair. J-Lo was setting a precedent, but was she starting a trend?

Paloma Picasso, one of the richest woman in the world, divorced her husband, Rafael Lopez-Chambil, after twenty-five years together. He reportedly asked for half her £500m fortune, a legacy from her artist father, Pablo, and her own business ventures. They finally settled out of court.

It is highly unlikely that there is any woman in this country who could afford to pay the kind of money that J-Lo did to end a marriage, and certainly there is no Irishwoman as wealthy as

Paloma Picasso. But the underlying principle behind these settlements could also apply here. Property and money may have to be shared equally on the break-up of a marriage, so if it is the woman in the marriage who is the one with the money, she must be prepared to pay up if she wants out of the partnership.

For the thousands of women going through the divorce courts every year, it is usually the other way around. It is normally the man who puts his hand in his pocket to pay the settlement. Most often, he is the person in the relationship who, by law, will have to pay maintenance to his wife and children. And he is usually the one who has to move out of the family home.

One thing is clear — money is an issue in a divorce settlement, no matter which partner has it.

But it is not the only one. The real cost to a divorcing couple is the emotional one. The reality of a divorce is that it can be the most traumatic event in the couple's life.

Who comes off worse? Statistics show that it is usually women who initiate divorce proceedings. But who suffers the most emotionally is debatable. It is a fact that, in the immediate aftermath of a divorce, a woman usually suffers less disruption — she generally stays where she is living and she is with the children. Nevertheless most woman are devastated by divorce.

'From what I have observed, women are the losers in a divorce,' a woman counsellor once told me. 'The reason most divorces are initiated by women is not because they want their freedom. They are disappointed because the marriage has been a failure for whatever reason. They haven't got what they wanted from that marriage. For women in their forties and fifties, divorce is catastrophic. It is much more difficult for women to embark on a new relationship, whereas a man of that age can — and often does — get a younger model, start a new family, begin again.'

The counsellor continued. 'While I know men can be broken-hearted by being separated from their children, I do feel they are much more adaptable at fitting in to new situations. And basically, they know they can find a new woman more easily than a woman of that age can find a man.'

'Elizabeth' would agree with her. Shortly before her silver wedding anniversary, she became a divorce statistic. She discovered that her husband was having an affair with her girlfriend, and that this had been going on for some time.

Her story is typical of many women who have to face the reality of a cheating husband. But the final confrontation is never easy.

'I was twenty when we married,' Elizabeth said. '"John" was twenty-one. We had our first child, a son, at the end of that year. A daughter followed a year later. Everything was fine for years. Or at least I thought it was. John was a good father. He adored the children.

'Things started to go wrong about ten years ago. John had an affair with a woman he met on a business trip. I suspected nothing for more than a year — as far as I was concerned, he really was away on business. I expected him to be faithful to me. Never, not for one moment, did I ever question what he was doing when he went away on those trips. When I did find out, the trust went completely from the relationship. Oh, we worked our way through it, but it was never the same . . . not for me, anyway.

'The marriage appeared to be plodding along ok. But then I began to recognise the signs . . . his evasiveness, particularly. This time, he was playing around nearer to home, with a close friend. I found that almost impossible to bear. How he could cheat on his own doorstep is beyond me, even now. It was unacceptable then, and it is now, particularly when he goes on and on about how much he loves her.

'Splitting up is never really something you think about when you have been married as long as we had. I expected to have a marriage as long as my parents did, to stick it out. But things were never the same for me after that.

'Yet, looking back, I probably would have hung on in there. It was John who wanted out. He thought his life was stale and boring. We'd reached the stage, with the children gone, when people settle down to grow old together. But it isn't like that any more because we are all living longer. John wanted fun, and he clearly thought he wasn't having it with me. As fed up with him as I was, the break-up was shattering. And four years later, I still feel cheated by it all. He has gone on to another younger woman, and he has a good relationship with our children. And me? I have no one. I devoted my life to him and the children — and what have I got to show for it? He's gone and the children are gone. I feel old before my time, and useless, really. No, I don't feel remotely liberated by the experience.'

'Jane', a successful, glamorous high-powered businesswoman, tells a completely different story. Jane is fifty, looks forty, has been divorced twice and is 'still looking for the love of my life'.

'In my first marriage, I was very young. So I was very young for a marriage to break up. I was only twenty-three. Breaking up was traumatic. When we married, I didn't even think about divorce. We had a separation agreement drawn up by my solicitor and as far as I was concerned, that was the end of the marriage. That was the way you thought about things then.

'It wasn't until years later, when I was having a relationship with someone else — the man I subsequently married — that I felt I had to take it a step further, because I presumed I would marry this man. I went and got a divorce in England . . . just so that I could feel better about things.

'I have to say that that divorce did not affect me at all. I was young; I didn't think about it. Second time around it was completely different. I was a stubborn sort of person, and determined, and the way I felt was that once the relationship was over . . . well, that was that. I don't have any regrets about that. But then, I was always very independent.

'Second-time-around was a different ball game. It was more difficult because I was older, and I suppose I had gone into that marriage for life. I really thought it was going to be long lasting. And I had one young child by then. So to walk away from a marriage where there was a young child was very, very difficult.

'We didn't divorce right away because of our daughter. Yet funnily enough, I wanted a divorce. Once he had gone, and once he didn't love me, I felt I wanted things tidied up. But it wasn't on the cards then.

'For me, it was the break-up of the marriage that caused the trauma, not the divorce. The divorce is just another piece of paper. OK, there is always one person who doesn't want the marriage to end, or maybe wants to work at it. But there is always one person who makes the decision at the end. Very few couples actually sit down and say "This is the end of the marriage for us". Very few have thought it out amicably. It just never happens like that. It's a pity it doesn't because that's the way it should be. But really, the break-up is the most emotional part of it.

'Why did we break up? He got bored with the marriage, and with me. It wasn't working for me either. It wasn't right; we had differences. I suppose we got on one another's nerves. It happens. There wasn't another woman. For me, the emotional trauma was being in the marriage when I knew it wasn't working. And then the actual split . . . yes, that was hell too.

'You don't walk away from a twelve-year marriage lightly, particularly one where you are convinced it is going to be all right.

'Now, I don't think it is any big deal. There are men out there, nice men. The only thing is, when you've lived with two men, you get fussy and choosy. And I do love my freedom and my independence. I suppose it helps that I am financially independent.

'Yet, I might, I just might marry again. I am still out there looking for Prince Charming. And you never know . . . '

Jane's case is unusual. Not many Irish women marry and divorce twice. But there is a trend towards second relationships after divorce, and they sometimes do end in marriage.

Internationally, the scene is quite different. Second and third marriages are common. But here and in other countries, the majority of marriage break-downs appear to occur in middle age. There is a definite trend towards middle-aged divorces and separations. This also applies to high-profile, long-duration couples.

The actress Lynn Redgrave left her husband, actor John Clark, after a 31-year marriage. Their marriage, billed as one of Hollywood's happiest, crumbled when she discovered that John had fathered a son by her daughter- in-law.

James Bond actor Roger Moore coughed up a whopping £10.5 million in a divorce settlement from his third wife, Luisa. Moore, now in his seventies, was married to her for twenty-five years, but had to wait six years for the divorce. Luisa, an

Italian actress in her sixties, claims he told her she was to be 'discarded' by phone.

Harrison Ford, the middle-aged and most highly paid actor in Hollywood, left his second wife, Melissa Mathison, last year. Ford had been married to Ms Mathison, the screenwriter of *ET*, for twenty years. He and *Ally McBeal* actor Calista Flockhart are now a regular item among the beautiful people in the US.

Another highly published middle-aged break up was that of Mick Jagger and Jerry Hall. She reportedly couldn't stand his infidelity any longer, but came out of the marriage £15 million richer. She now claims to be blissfully happy with Tim Attias.

While we all get to hear about the financial settlements of international celebrity couples, we rarely, if ever, know the details when our own rich-and-famous split. Although wealthy Dublin businessman Michael Smurfit split from his then wife Norma many years ago and went on to remarry and break up from another woman, the details of his break-up from his first wife were never in the public domain.

Show business people tend to be more open about their marriage break-ups, as was the case when TV personality Mike Murphy split from his wife Eileen after a marriage of many years. She eventually spoke openly to the press about their break-up, although he was more reticent.

In the case of the marriage break-ups of middle-aged couples, the trend appears to be for men to move on into other relationships. A case in point is the current Minister for Finance, Charlie McCreevy, who is in a second marriage and lives with his wife, Noeleen, in Co. Kildare.

But even in less high-profile cases, it would appear that it is the man who moves out of the marriage and quickly into another relationship. Are men less able to sustain a marriage? Or are they just fickle at heart?

Acclaimed psychiatrist Dr Anthony Clare, author of *On Men, Masculinity in Crisis*, has said that the escalating depredations of divorce are partly due to our attitude to adultery. 'Anglo-Saxon culture is both permissive and punitive in its view of infidelity. If one partner strays, you see the whole relationship fall apart, which perhaps it needn't. I think the tolerant Latin approach is more realistic.'

But Dr Clare has claimed that men are not puppets to their hormones. Of the demon testosterone, blamed for wife battering and football carnage, most molesters, abusers and candidates for chemical castration have no testosterone imbalance at all. On the contrary, Dr Clare claims that testosterone levels rise in athletes before performances, suggesting that the body produces it in anticipation of events and emotions; it is therefore an aid to aggression, not a cause of it.

In his book, Dr Clare suggests that women are the ones with the better deal in mid life.

'Now at the start of the 2000s, I don't see so many women from empty nests. Rather I see middle-aged men who gave their lives loyally to this company or that corporation, who sacrificed everything for it, now put out to grass, retired, downsized, rendered redundant. It is the women who now play the golf, who have jobs and friends at work. It is the men who cower in the empty nest, nervously facing the forgotten future.'

Dr Clare describes his own marriage: 'As a young husband, I loved my wife and was, I believe, a sympathetic and liberated "new" male. Nowadays, I am not so sure. She sacrificed much to be a committed and full-time mother. I sacrificed little to be a peripheral and very part-time dad. But I was the family provider and that counted for a great deal — to me at any rate — and I was a father to my children, even if I was hard put to define precisely what being a father was.'

Not all men are as lucky in a marriage. And when a marriage breaks up, some men, particularly younger ones, are prepared to talk about it.

'Michael' is an electrician who lives in the country. He too did his own divorce after five years of marriage because he wanted matters tied up. He wanted to start afresh with his new partner, 'Ann', the mother of his child.

'Maybe I should have persevered in the marriage, but really, there was nothing to go on with. We were too young when we got married and if you talked to my ex wife, she would say the same. I wish I could say that it was her infidelity, or my drinking, that broke up the marriage, but it was nothing like that. We simply didn't have a relationship at the end of it. There was no sex between us, but equally, there was no companionship.'

Now in his late thirties, Michael says Ann was not the cause of his marriage break-up. 'I had already left the relationship when I met Ann, and she was the best thing that happened to me. It is just so easy being with her — nothing is a problem or an issue. We even figured out together how to do my divorce.'

But they also asked for, and got, help from Gay Gaynor, the subject of this book, in compiling the divorce papers.

'The whole thing went well from the start. I didn't find it that difficult to do. Our solicitor was sceptical about my doing it, but in the end, I think he actually admired me taking it on.'

Michael only made one mistake at the outset of doing his own divorce He thought that he had to bring the divorce papers to Dublin, when in fact the papers had to be served in his own area.

'But the girls in the Dublin court offices were really terrific. They couldn't have been nicer. They looked at the papers but they explained that it had to be done at our local offices. So we had to start all over again.

'The girls in the court in Dublin actually went to the trouble of sending our papers to our local office. Then the girls in our office phoned to tell us that everything was in order. The only thing we had to do was get a sworn affidavit saying why we had made the mistake of taking them to Dublin in the first place.

'The amazing thing is that there was no surprise from anyone at our local court that we were doing our own divorce.'

The day that Michael went to court for his divorce, his partner Ann did not go with him. This was the one event in his life that she felt she did not want to be involved with. She felt Michael had to handle this on his own.

The day that Michael went for his divorce, he was part of a huge group involved in family law cases. His ex wife was there, though as Michael says: 'She didn't have to be. Once I had sent her the

Civil Bill, the affidavits, and she had sent them all back to me, having agreed to them and signed them, she really didn't have to be there. But it worked out ok. It was all very amicable. Ours was a very straight-forward divorce; there were no children involved, and our relationship had got to the stage where there was nowhere else to go.

'On that day in that courthouse, we sat in a room until roll call. There were about twenty-two couples in all. I was number twelve on the list. There was one judge and about seven clerks. The judge came in and asked us our names, separately. He asked my ex wife if she had come of her own free will; how long we were separated; and whether the legal end of it had been sorted.

'From the time I walked into the courthouse until I walked out, the whole process took about five to six minutes. When I thought the whole thing was over and done with, the judge asked me whether I needed a "blocking order". I didn't know what he meant, so he explained that once he imposed this order, that neither of us could claim anything further from the other again. He made the order then and there.

'The sense of relief I experienced after that was amazing. There is a terrific finality about divorce, which there just isn't about a legal separation.'

Not every man would agree with Michael about that 'sense of relief'. 'Karl' is one of them.

An alcoholic who is not drinking at the moment, Karl lives on his own and has done since his wife left him after a lifetime of tolerating his moods of depression, elation, bullying, and what she claims was 'his totally destructive behaviour generally'. His wife, 'Ruth', has moved on, is with another man and instigated and got a divorce from him earlier this year.

'I hate being divorced,' says Karl. 'And I hated being separated. I just like things being the way they were. I suppose that is selfish of me? Of course it is.

'When I was sober, I wondered how she had tolerated me, but when I was drinking, I just felt she had let me down; she should have stayed in the marriage, should have seen it through.'

Karl is the father of three children and he and Ruth were together for twenty-six years. 'The break-up of our marriage has damaged the children. But then, if I am honest, my drinking did too. It damaged me, and it damaged my wife. There was never a moment when I didn't love those kids and want to be with them, but the pub always seemed a happier place for me. I feel now that they must hate me, because now that they are adults, they must feel I abandoned them. I know I wasn't there for all the important things in their lives — the big events and the small everyday things.

'My wife was mother and father to them. She supplied all the material and emotional support to them.

'I would never have chosen for the marriage to break up, but you know, before the divorce, I really thought she would come back to me. There is an awful finality about divorce. I know the kids feel that too, but kids are resilient . . . they are moving on.

'I suppose I am lucky that my wife stayed with me as long as she did. Years ago, that's what wives did. They really put up with everything. At first, I didn't think I was a bad husband. Everyone drank then, and most men that I knew were heavy drinkers. I never kept her short of money, but it's not enough. I was never there, really. She says I bullied her. I don't think I did — I never hit her.

'I wasn't promiscuous, although most drinkers are, so she can't say I was unfaithful to her. None of that matters now, though, now that she is gone.'

Karl says he will continue to live alone, and that his main pleasure in life now are visits from his children. His hope is that eventually, they will understand and forgive him.

That hope is shared by the many thousand 'weekend dads' around the country.

Part–time fathers may be seen as the casualties of divorce, but the real losers in most cases are the children.

A survey conducted in Britain some time ago found that children from broken homes were almost twice as likely to have underage sex as those living with both parents. Researchers for the Family Education Trust, a group that campaigns for traditional family values, found that 25% of children of divorced or separated couples had engaged in underage sex, compared with 13% of those whose parents were married or cohabiting.

Yet another survey conducted in Britain, based on international research spanning thirty years, found that children of separated families were more likely to:

- Leave school with low educational qualifications
- Leave home when young
- Experience early sexual activity and unmarried teenage pregnancy
- Display withdrawn behaviour, aggression, substance abuse and delinquency
- Suffer depression in adolescence and adulthood
- Earn low pay and be unemployed as adults

While these statistics may not apply here, more and more children are nevertheless becoming the casualties of broken marriages. One counsellor told me that in a group of bereaved children she was overseeing, three-quarters of them were not there because of the death of a parent, but because of the trauma they were suffering from the break-up of their parents' marriages. They too were grieving for the loss of a parent.

'In one way, they were more pathetic than the children who had lost a parent. These children had really low self-esteem, much more so than the children whose father or mother had died. And they felt so ashamed, as if they were to blame for their parents' break-up. They were really sad little people.'

There are more losers than winners when a couple goes down the divorce route — a fact which makes many couples hesitate before taking that final step. It could be the reason why Irish Taoiseach Bertie Ahern has consistently ruled out divorce from his separated wife, Miriam, and it could be the reason why she has not insisted on a divorce, even though he is seen publicly in a relationship with his partner, Celia Larkin.

But despite all the drawbacks, tensions and trauma associated with divorce, the majority of people who end up in the divorce courts agree it was worth it. Having that divorce paper in their hands opens the way to a new life, maybe even to a new partner.

And, if they are very lucky, to the chance of love the second time around.

In the first-person accounts quoted above, all the names have been changed for legal reasons.

A DIY DIVORCE

'While we were outside the Family Court, waiting to be called in for our divorce hearing, I couldn't help noticing the other people with their barristers and solicitors. We were the only people representing ourselves. The others had probably forked out thousands on legal fees — and here we were, spending about €25 on our divorce. Yet we were the two having a laugh while most of the couples we saw that day seemed so hostile towards each other . . .'

Gay Gaynor, then a Dublin secretary in her early thirties, organised her own divorce in 1999. Gay is proud of her achievement. Somehow, she feels that she has managed to beat the legal system, a system which she believes is stacked against the ordinary man or woman who can't afford the exorbitant legal fees involved in a divorce case.

Gay and Brendan Gaynor are among more than 13,000 couples who have applied for divorce since the introduction of the Family Law (Divorce) Act in 1997. (The Act itself was passed on 27 November 1996 but didn't come into effect until 27 February 1997.) According to the Dublin Courts Service, women applicants outnumber men. Both in divorce and judicial separation (as an alternative to divorce), women outnumber men by five-to-one.

When Professor Gabriel Kiely of the Family Study Centre, UCD, conducted his own pilot study of 100 people whose marriages had broken down, he discovered that not everyone goes through a divorce when a marriage breaks up.

'There is no evidence to support the view that everyone is rushing into divorce. In Ireland, separation is seen as an exit, while divorce is considered an entry to a new relationship. In Italy, too, another largely Catholic country, a legal separation is viewed as an exit from the relationship, and divorce the entry to the new partnership. In other jurisdictions like the US and Britain, divorce is the exit. There's a cultural dimension to it here — even though they may be separated, many couples still see themselves as being married.'

In his study, conducted by post with couples he had located through the various support groups for separated people (like Gingerbread, AIM and Separated Parents), Professor Kiely learned that couples whose marriages had broken down had used a variety of ways to sort out their difficulties. Some went through the Government Mediation Service. Some made their own informal arrangements. Still others had obtained a legal separation using a solicitor.

For the nearly 3,500 couples who went through divorce in the year 2001, it was usually a costly business. A survey conducted by the Dublin Solicitors' Bar Association found that, for marital breakdown cases, solicitors' fees alone amount to an average of €6,350, plus vat, for each couple. If a case is heard in court, total costs can exceed €19,000. This, of course, is in addition to the costs involved in selling the family home and dividing its contents, the maintenance of dependent children, custody and access, accountancy costs . . . the list continues. There are significant hidden costs as well, such as estate agents' fees and pension advice.

This kind of money was out of the question for Gay Gayner. Yet she was determined to get a divorce. With her husband Brendan's agreement, Gay set about interpreting the new divorce legislation to suit her own needs.

This is the story of how an ordinary woman, a mother of two, got her own divorce. Assisted only by the staff at the Family Law Courts — assistance which Gay acknowledges with gratitude — she figured out how to make up her own divorce papers. After a few false starts, the papers she ultimately presented in court met all the necessary legal requirements.

From the time of her first dealings with the staff in the Family Law Courts until her actual day in court, the whole procedure took about six weeks.

And it cost her about €25.00.

While others may have been successful in representing themselves in court in divorce proceedings, Gay Gaynor hopes that, by telling her story and outlining the details of her legal struggles, other men and women will have the courage to do what she did. In doing so, she believes they can avoid much of the trauma and heartache — and the high costs — associated with divorce. In a practical way, Gay feels that this book will act as a guide to couples seeking divorce.

Though there is trauma associated with most divorces or separations, there is life after divorce. Gay Gaynor is now in a happy second relationship, has in fact just got engaged and plans a second marriage in the Spring.

GAY'S STORY

She was so excited when she heard the judge say 'You're divorced' that she couldn't contain herself. When she got outside, Gay punched the air in triumph.

She knew Brendan was pleased too. He was kissing her and hugging her — actually thanking her for everything. He even complimented her on how well she was bringing up their two children as a single parent.

Standing in front of the judge at the Riverbank Courthouse, Gay had been extremely nervous. She loved that old part of the city near Dublin Castle and felt an affinity with it. Yet she was anxious, as was Brendan. They both wondered how the judge would react to them doing their own divorce.

Gay had dressed carefully and conservatively for the occasion. She wore black from head to toe because she wanted to be taken seriously. Although Brendan had chosen to wear jeans, he looked smart, his shirt expertly pressed.

Upon entering the court, Gay informed the clerk that she and Brendan were representing themselves. Then, all they could do was wait outside the courthouse until their names were called.

As they did so, Gay couldn't help letting her mind wander back over the past.

When she married Brendan, she was in love. Now, however, Gay realised they had been too young when they got married. She herself was only 22 at the time while Brendan was 21.

After seven years, Gay could see that the marriage wasn't working. She and Brendan weren't communicating . . . they wanted different things. More or less at the same time, both of them came to the same conclusion: they should separate. Gay was relieved, glad that they weren't bickering over it. Their legal separation followed as a matter of course.

Still, she was only 29 years old and Gay felt there was unfinished business. She had a lot of living to do and she wanted things tidied up.

She wanted a divorce.

Gay went to a solicitor and was told that a divorce would cost her around €3,100, with another €3,100 for her husband. Although neither she nor Brendan had that kind of money, Gay was sure that she would find a way to get a divorce.

It was at this point that Gay decided to organise her own divorce. She had heard that people sometimes represented themselves in court, so why couldn't she?

First, Gay set about finding the booklet, *Circuit Court Rules (Number 1)*. She wrote to the Government Publications Office and discovered that she could buy it for about €7.60. With the book in front of her, she started reading . . . and she couldn't understand a word of it.

It was a year and a half before Gay tackled the book again — and this time, she studied it over and over again for eight solid months.

Referring to the book, Gay drew up every conceivable type of document that would be needed in her divorce case. These documents were her versions of the ones in this book, and she applied her own personal circumstances to each one.

With the documents completed to the best of her ability, Gay took them to the Family Law Courts in Dublin. Although she didn't have an appointment, the staff members were patient and kind, providing her with further direction and guiding her through the papers she had already drawn up.

Each document required Gay to provide different types of information. In the *Family Law Civil Bill*, for example, Gay had to specify: when she was married; why her marriage had broken down; details of where they both lived; what was happening to the family home. In the *Affidavit of Means*, she had to compile lists (known as *Schedules*) of what monies were incoming and outgoing, including details of debts and pensions. The clerks at the Family Law Courts told her that every document needed a front cover and that she must keep a record of every time she gave her husband a certain document.

Gay's first attempts were disasters. Everything had to be redone. For her, the most difficult document to prepare was the *Affidavit of Welfare* which dealt with the welfare of her children. She had to describe who looked after the children on a daily basis; say how many bedrooms she had; whether there were children from another relationship; whether the children went to a State or a fee-paying school; whether they had any special education or health needs. As with the other documents, Gay didn't get it right at first.

Even though Gay was discovering aspects of the law which she never knew existed — or never thought she could understand — her task was made easier because her husband, Brendan, was co-operating with her all the way. If he had not agreed, however — had he not appeared in court or acknowledged the receipt of documents — she could have sent him a letter stating that she was going to apply to the court for Judgment by Default. In her case, since she and Brendan had been living apart for four out of the previous five years, she would have been able to go ahead with the divorce without his co-operation. Gay's case was made more simple because both parties had agreed to the divorce.

Gay's court date was scheduled on her third appearance in the offices of the Family Law Courts. It was for 14 January 1999. From the time Gay had started her own divorce proceedings, the whole experience had taken a little more than six weeks.

As Gay and her soon-to-be ex-husband Brendan went into court, she was calm. As she had initiated proceedings, she had to stand in the witness box and swear on the Bible that the statements she was about to make were true. When the judge asked her questions about the children and other aspects of the agreements, she was able to answer confidently. She didn't feel intimidated. The judge asked her how the children were coping, whether their father had access to them and whether Brendan paid maintenance. While the children were coping well and there was no problem with access, Brendan was not paying maintenance. But this was the way she wanted it. Gay stated that she was working and that she wanted to stand on her own two feet, to keep herself and support her children.

When Gay had recovered from the relief and excitement of getting her divorce, she and Brendan went for a drink in a pub in Dublin's Capel Street. A drink led to lunch in Abbey Street, followed by a day of reminiscences. Happiness and relief were tinged with sadness at the thought of the bad times, the boredom she had experienced in a marriage that hadn't worked.

By the time she had parted from Brendan after one of the most important days of her life, Gay felt sure of one thing: she may have lost a husband, but she had gained a friend for life.

Divorce cases are no longer dealt with at River-bank Courthouse. The divorce court now operates from an address at Phoenix House, Phoenix Street, Smithfield, Dublin.

FOLLOWING THE RULES

This is a step-by-step guide to how Gay Gaynor went about getting her own divorce. The facts that she had been separated for seven years and already had a legal separation were contributing factors to her success. In addition, her husband Brendan was co-operating with her, and there was no argument about money since Gay didn't want any monetary settlement. She successfully requested that their council house be put in her name and she is now buying it from the County Council.

Gay also didn't want any child support. As she was working, she felt strongly about wanting to support her children herself.

Although Gay and Brendan were legally separated, a legal separation is not required prior to getting a divorce. If a couple has lived apart for four consecutive years, they can file for divorce. Once the

Applicant (the person who initiates divorce proceedings) has served the initial papers, the *Respondent* (the person who must respond to these papers) has 10 working days in which to reply. If the Respondent disagrees with the divorce, s/he has 20 working days in which to make their case to the courts in writing. Grounds for contesting the divorce must be reasonable and responsible. If the Respondent is resident outside the State, s/he is allowed 30 working days to contest the divorce.

The Documents

As the Applicant — the person who is applying for the divorce — you will need the following documents when you appear in court. They cover all aspects of the process: whether or not the couple has children; whether or not maintenance is being sought; when the spouse is living outside the State.

- *Family Law Civil Bill* — 3 copies (1 each for Applicant, Respondent and court)
- *Affidavit of Means* — 2 copies (for Applicant and court). The Respondent does not receive a copy of this.
- *Affidavit of Welfare* (only if you have children under 23 years of age) — 3 copies (1 each for Applicant, Respondent and court)

- *Affidavit of Service* — 1 copy
- *Notice of Motion* — 3 copies (1 each for Applicant, Respondent and court)
- *Service of Motion* — 1 copy

The following documents must be sworn by a solicitor:

- *Affidavit of Means*
- *Affidavit of Welfare*
- *Affidavit of Service*
- *Service of Motion*

These documents are not all sworn at the same time.

In some circumstances, the following documents may be needed:

- *Ex Parte Document* — If the Respondent resides outside the Republic of Ireland
- *Certificate of No Appearance* — If the Respondent does not reply to the above documents
- *Notice to Trustees* — If either person wishes to make a claim on a pension scheme(s), this notice must be presented to the trustees of pension scheme(s) held by either the Applicant or Respondent.

You also need a copy of your *Marriage Certificate* and, if you have one, a copy of your *Separation Agreement*.

The Steps

Gay Gaynor believes that anyone who follows these steps and prepares their documents as she did should be able to get their own divorce without incurring costly legal fees. Like Gay, you may have to redo the documents a few times. In doing so, however, Gay herself became more and more confident. And she succeeded.

Remember to keep copies of everything for your files — too many copies are better than too few. A well-organised filing system is also recommended, as is a diary in which to keep a record of when each document was completed, witnessed, posted etc.

1. Prepare the *Family Law Civil Bill* (pages 39–44), the *Affidavit of Means* (pages 45–49) and the *Affidavit of Welfare* (pages 51–58). The *Affidavit of Welfare* is required only when there are children aged 23 and under.

2. Get the relevant number of copies of each document (see page 32).

3. The *Affidavit of Means* and *Affidavit of Welfare* must be sworn by a solicitor. This should cost between €3.80–€5.00 per document.

4. Bring the completed copies of the *Family Law Civil Bill*, the *Affidavit of Means* and the *Affidavit of Welfare* to your local courthouse offices to lodge your claim for divorce. Inform the staff that you are doing your own divorce. A staff member will take these documents and stamp them. The court will keep one copy of the *Family Law Civil Bill*, the *Affidavit of Means* and the *Affidavit of Welfare*. They will return the other copies to you. These are now legal documents and should never be altered in any way.

5. Now that the documents have been stamped, give or send your spouse (the Respondent) a copy of the stamped *Family Law Civil Bill* and the *Affidavit of Welfare*. This can be done personally, although registered post is preferrable. Keep the posting receipt for your files.

6. In addition to the documents in 5 above, you must also send your spouse a letter stating that you intend seeking a divorce within 14 days of his/her receipt of these papers. In this letter, state that your spouse now has 10 working

days in which to give/send you a dated, *hand-written letter* stating that s/he will agree to the divorce under 'no contest'. Keep copies of these documents for your files.

NOTE: If your spouse/the Respondent ignores any of the papers which are sent to him/her, you will need the *Certificate of No Appearance* (page 77) which asks the court for a *Judgment by Default*.

7. Prepare your *Affidavit of Service*. Fill in the relevant dates, stating when you gave/sent your spouse the *Family Law Civil Bill*. Get the relevant number of copies (see page 32). The *Affidavit of Service* must also be sworn by a solicitor at a cost of €3.80–€5.00.

8. Once the Respondent has given you the dated, hand-written letter stating that s/he will agree to the divorce, s/he need not appear in court until the final court day. Keep a copy of this letter in your files.

9. Prepare your *Notice of Motion* (page 63) and — even though it may not be needed — your *Certificate of No Appearance* (page 77).

10. When 10 working days are up (or 20 days, if the divorce is being contested), return to the courthouse offices with the following:

- the *Affidavit of Service*
- the *hand-written letter from your spouse*
- the *Certificate of No Appearance*
- the *Notice of Motion*

The *Affidavit of Service*, the *hand-written letter* and the *Certificate of No Appearance* will be filed with the court. The *Notice of Motion* will be filled in by the court staff.

11. When the *Notice of Motion* is filled in and stamped by the court staff, give/send your spouse a copy of this document. It is notification of your date and time in court.

12. Fill in your *Service of Motion* document. This states when you gave your spouse his/her copy of the *Notice of Motion*. This document must also be sworn by a solicitor at a cost of €3.80–€5.00. Bring this, and all your other documents, to your court hearing.

13. When your court date arrives, you must be at the court *at least* 15 minutes earlier than stated on your *Notice of Motion*. Proceed to the court numbered on your *Notice of Motion*. Inform the Clerk of the Court that you have arrived and tell him/her that you are representing yourself in court. H/She will ask the

names of both parties and tell you to wait outside until your case is called.

14. When your names are called, you and your spouse will be the only people allowed in the courtroom. You (the Applicant) will then stand in the witness box and swear on the Bible to the truth of your statements. The judge will ask a number of questions: whether both parties are in agreement; whether there are children of the marriage and how they are being looked after etc. Once the judge is satisfied with these responses, s/he will make the final ruling.

15. Approximately 7 working days after your court hearing, return to the offices of the court. Inform the staff of the date of your previous appearance and tell them that you are now here to obtain your final *Divorce Papers*. Get 4 copies of these and return them to the offices of the court. These copies must be original typed copies. They must NOT be photocopies. Two copies will go on file and two will be returned to you.

16. The couple is now divorced.

Some courts around the 26 counties differ slightly, with a premilinary hearing prior to the actual divorce hearing.

FAMILY LAW CIVIL BILL

This is the most important document in your divorce papers. When the spouse (Respondent) receives it, s/he has the opportunity to agree with it or contest the proceedings.

If this document is ignored by the Respodent, proceedings may still go ahead without further notice.

Three copies are required — 1 each for the Applicant, the Respondent and the court. A cover page (page 41) is also needed.

The Family Civil Law Bill sets out the following points in the section called *Indorsement of Claim*:

- The date of the marriage
- The residency status of both parties
- The current address of both parties
- Children of the marriage (if any)

- The reasons why the marriage broke up
- When the separation occurred
- The date of the legal separation (if any)
- The current status of the family home

Each of these points must be set out in separate, numbered paragraphs.

The Applicant should also set out clearly what s/he is looking for in the divorce — financial settlements etc. Although Gay Gaynor did not seek a financial settlement, many couples will. Details of their agreed arrangements should be set out clearly and precisely in Section 10.

While the Applicant's claim will obviously differ in each case, the sample document on pages 41–44 provides a general presentation.

(This is the Sample Cover Page for the Family Law Civil Bill)

AN CHUIRT TEAGHLAIGH CHUARDA
(THE CIRCUIT FAMILY COURT)

(Insert Circuit Court Name) **CIRCUIT** **COUNTY OF** *(Insert county name)*

IN THE MATTER OF THE FAMILY LAW
(DIVORCE) ACT, 1996

BETWEEN *(Insert name of person applying for divorce)*
Applicant

AND

(Insert name of spouse, the person who is responding)
Respondent

FAMILY LAW CIVIL BILL

FORM No. 1
AN CHUIRT TEAGHLAIGH CHUARDA
(THE CIRCUIT FAMILY COURT)

(*Insert Circuit Court Name*)   **CIRCUIT**   **COUNTY OF** (*Insert county name*)
IN THE MATTER OF THE FAMILY LAW (DIVORCE) ACT, 1996

BETWEEN   (*Insert name of person applying for divorce*)
                                           Applicant
                                                 AND
          (*Insert name of spouse, the person who is responding*)
                                      Respondent

FAMILY LAW CIVIL BILL

You are hereby required within ten days after the service of this Civil Bill upon you, to enter, or cause to be entered with the County Registrar, at his or her office at (***Insert the address of your local Family Court here***) an appearance to answer the Claim of (***Insert the Applicant's name and address here***), the Applicant herein as indorsed hereon.

AND TAKE NOTICE THAT unless you do enter an Appearance, you will be held to have admitted the said claim and the Applicant may proceed therein and judgment may be given against you in your absence without further notice.

AND FURTHER TAKE NOTICE THAT if you intend to defend the proceedings on any grounds, you must not only enter an Appearance as aforesaid, but also within ten days after the Appearance deliver a statement in writing showing the nature and grounds of your Defence.

The Appearance and Defence may be entered by posting same to the said Office and by giving copies to the Applicant and/or his/her Solicitor by post.

Dated the (*Date*) day of (*Month*) 20??

Signed: (***Signature of Applicant goes here***)
                                   (*Typed Name of Applicant*)
                                   APPLICANT

To: (*Name of Respondent*)
     (*Address of Respondent*)

INDORSEMENT OF CLAIM
(Sample)

1. The Applicant and the Respondent were married on the *(Insert date and place of marriage here)*.

2. The Applicant and the Respondent are both Irish Citizens and have resided within the State for the year prior to the institution of these proceedings.

3. The Applicant resides at *(Insert address and occupation here)*.

4. The Respondent resides at *(Insert address and occupation here)*.

5. There was an issue of the marriage, namely: *(List children's names and their dates of birth here).*

6. Throughout the marriage, the relationship deteriorated between the Applicant and the Respondent with a complete breakdown in communication such that the Applicant and Respondent began living separately.

7. The Applicant and the Respondent lived separate and apart since in or around *(Insert date of separation)* and no normal marital relationship has existed since that date. The Applicant and the Respondent have been separated in excess of 4 years out of the previous five years prior to the institution of these proceedings and the marriage has broken down to the extent that there is no possibility of reconciliation.

8. The Family home is situated at *(Insert address here)* and is held in the name of *(Insert the name of owner; whether it is rented or owned; whether it is subject to a mortgage or rental agreement with the County Council or Corporation)*.

   (If you have a legal seperation, insert the following, Point 9. Attach a copy of the Separation Agreement to this document.)

9. Pursuant to a legal separation/separation agreement signed by the parties on *(Insert date here)*, all matters of custody, maintenance, finances, property *(delete where necessary)* have been agreed between the parties, a copy of which is annexed hereto.

0. *(Details of financial settlements should be agreed prior to submitting this document. Set them out clearly and precisely here.)*

AND THE APPLICANT'S CLAIM IS FOR: *(EXAMPLE)*

1. A Decree of Divorce pursuant to the provisions of Section 5 (1) of the Family Law (Divorce) Act.
2. An Order and a cross order pursuant to the provisions of Section 18 (10) of the Family Law (Divorce) Act 1996, that neither the Applicant nor the Respondent herein shall, on the death of the other, be entitled to apply for provision out of the Estate of the other herein pursuant to the provisions of the said section.

AND TAKE FURTHER NOTICE that, in cases where financial relief is sought by either party, you must file with the Defence herein or in any event within 20 days after the service of the Civil Bill upon you at the aforementioned Circuit Court Office an Affidavit of Means and, where appropriate, an Affidavit of Welfare in the Manner prescribed by the Rules of this Court and serve a copy of same as provided by the Rules of this Court on the Applicant or his/her Solicitor at the address provided below.

Dated the *(Date)* day of *(Month)* 20??

The address for services of proceedings upon the Applicant is as follows:

(Insert address of Applicant)

Signed: *(Applicant's signature)*

_____

(Insert typed name of Applicant)
Applicant

To: The Registrar   And: *(Name of Respondent)*
    Circuit Family Court   *(Address of Respondent)*
    (Insert local address here)

TAKE NOTICE that it is in your interest to have legal advice in regard to these proceedings. If you cannot afford a private solicitor, you may be entitled to legal aid provided by the State at a minimum cost to you. Details of this legal aid service are available at the following address:

Legal Aid Board
47 Upper Mount Street
Dublin 2   Tel: 01 661 5811

where you can obtain the addresses and telephone numbers of the Legal Aid Centres in your area.

AFFIDAVIT OF MEANS

This document sums up the outgoings and income of the Applicant. It must be sworn by a solicitor. Two copies are needed — one for the Applicant and one for the court. A title page is required.

Points 1 to 6 (page 47) cannot be changed, either by the Applicant or the Respondent. These statements are sworn under oath and *must be copied exactly as shown*.

In Schedules one to five (see page 48), the Applicant must set out:

- First Schedule — All personal assets
- Second Schedule — Sources of income
- Third Schedule — Debts and/or Liabilities
- Fourth Schedule — Weekly personal outgoings
- Fifth Schedule — Details of a pension(s) scheme (if any)

(This is the Sample Cover Page for the Affidavit of Means)

AN CHUIRT TEAGHLAIGH CHUARDA

(THE CIRCUIT FAMILY COURT)

(Insert Circuit Court Name) **CIRCUIT**   **COUNTY OF** *(Insert county name)*

IN THE MATTER OF THE FAMILY LAW (DIVORCE) ACT, 1996

BETWEEN   *(Insert name of person applying for divorce)*
Applicant

AND

(Insert name of spouse, the person who is responding)
Respondent

AFFIDAVIT OF MEANS

FORM NO. 2

AN CHUIRT TEAGHLAIGH CHUARDA
(THE CIRCUIT FAMILY COURT)

(Insert Circuit Court Name) **CIRCUIT**   **COUNTY OF** *(Insert county name)*

IN THE MATTER OF THE FAMILY LAW (DIVORCE) ACT, 1996

BETWEEN
(Insert name of person applying for divorce)
Applicant

AND

(Insert name of spouse, the person who is responding)
Respondent

AFFIDAVIT OF MEANS

I, *(Insert Name, Address and Occupation of Applicant here)*, aged 18 years and upwards MAKE OATH and say as follows:

1. I say that I am the Applicant/Respondent *(delete as appropriate)* in the above entitled proceedings and I make this Affidavit from facts within my own knowledge save where otherwise appears and where so appearing I believe the same to be true.

2. I say that I have set out in the First Schedule hereto all the assets to which I am legally or beneficially entitled and the manner in which such property is held.

3. I say that I have set out in the Second Schedule hereto all income which I receive and the source(s) of such income.

4. I say that I have set out in the Third Schedule hereto all my debts and/or liabilities and the persons to whom such debts and liabilities are due.

5. I say that my weekly outgoings amount to the sum of € *(Insert weekly outgoings/ expenses here)* and I say that the details of such outgoings have been set out in the Fourth Schedule hereto.

6. I say that to the best of my knowledge, information and belief, all pension information known to me relevant to the within proceedings is set out in the Fifth Schedule hereto. [Where information has been obtained from the trustees of the pension scheme concerned under the Pensions Act, 1990, such information should be exhibited and where such information has not beenobtained, the Deponent should depose to the reason(s) why such information has not been obtained.]

FIRST SCHEDULE
ASSETS OF APPLICANT

(List all assets here in Euro)

SECOND SCHEDULE
INCOME OF APPLICANT

1.	Weekly wage	€000.00
2.	Children's allowance	€000.00
	Total	**€000.00**

THIRD SCHEDULE
DEBTS AND/OR LIABILITIES OF APPLICANT

(Insert any debts here — Mortgage, Credit Union loan, Bank loan etc.)

FOURTH SCHEDULE
WEEKLY PERSONAL OUTGOINGS OF APPLICANT

1.	Food	€80.00
2.	Mortgage	€25.00
3.	ESB	€12.00
4.	Gas	€12.00
5.	Phone	€12.00
6.	Cable	€15.00
7.	Insurance	€12.00
8.	Miscellaneous	€65.00
	Total:	**€233.00**

FIFTH SCHEDULE
PENSION SCHEME DETAILS

(Insert all pension details here)

DECLARED before me by the said

(Insert your name here)

who is personally known to me
(or who is identified to me by)

At *(Insert location/address)*

This *(date)* day of *(month)*, 20??

_____

Commissioner For Oaths/Practising Solicitor

Signed:_____

(Type your name here)
Applicant

AFFIDAVIT OF WELFARE

This document, which must be sworn by a solicitor, is required when there are dependent children of the marriage (children under the age of 23). Where maintenance is involved, this is normally agreed between the divorcing parties beforehand or through the courts prior to divorce proceedings.

Three copies are needed, as well as a title page.

All details of the children of this marriage, or of children from previous or current relationships, must be provided here. These details should include the addresses at which the children live, who owns the house where the children live, who lives there with the children, and their relationship with the children. All details should be given here: eg the names of the children's schools and whether these are fee-paying schools.

Child-care details must be included: eg who looks after the children? There is a section dealing with maintenance from the Respondent (if any), and whether s/he has contact with the children, and how often. Details should be included about the health of the parents and the children. If any of them is suffering from a serious illness, details should be given about medical care and how that care is provided.

If the children are involved in any court proceedings and there are relevant documents, these documents must be attached to this document.

Some of the following questions do not include sample answers as they are straightforward. Simply answer them as they apply to your own circumstances.

(This is the Sample Cover Page for the Affidavit of Welfare)

AN CHUIRT TEAGHLAIGH CHUARDA
(THE CIRCUIT FAMILY COURT)

(Insert Circuit Court Name) CIRCUIT   COUNTY OF *(Insert county name)*

IN THE MATTER OF THE FAMILY LAW (DIVORCE) ACT, 1996

BETWEEN   *(Insert name of person applying for divorce)*
Applicant

AND

(Insert name of spouse, the person who is responding)
Respondent

AFFIDAVIT OF WELFARE

FORM No. 3

AN CHUIRT TEAGHLAIGH CHUARDA
(THE CIRCUIT FAMILY COURT)

(Insert Circuit Court Name) **CIRCUIT**   **COUNTY OF** *(Insert county name)*

IN THE MATTER OF THE FAMILY LAW (DIVORCE) ACT, 1996

BETWEEN   *(Insert name of person applying for divorce)*
Applicant

AND

(Insert name of spouse, the person who is responding)
Respondent

AFFIDAVIT OF WELFARE

I, *(Insert your name, address and occupation here)*, aged 18 years and upwards
MAKE OATH and say as follows:

1. I say that I am the Applicant/Resondent *(Delete as appropriate)* in the above
entitled proceedings and I make this Affidavit from facts within my own
knowledge save where otherwise appears and where so appearing I believe the
same to be true.

2. I say and believe that the facts set out in the Schedule hereto are true.

[In circumstances in which the Respondent does not dispute the facts as deposed to
by the Applicant in his/her Affidavit of Welfare, the following averment shall be
included, replacing Paragraph 2 hereof, and in such circumstances, the Schedule shall
not be completed by the Respondent.]

3. I say that I am fully in agreement with the facts as averred to by the Applicant in
his/her Affidavit of Welfare sworn herein on the *(Insert date)* day of *(Insert
month)* 20xx and I say and believe that the facts set out in the Schedule thereto are
true.

SCHEDULE
Part I — Details of the Children

1. Details of children born to the Applicant and the Respondent or adopted by both the Applicant and the Respondent.

Forenames   **Surnames**   **Dates of Birth**

2. Details of other children of the family or to which the parties or either of them are in loco parentis.

(If you have any children from a previous or current relationship, insert names and dates of birth here. The term 'in loco parentis' means 'in place of the parent'.)

Forenames   **Surnames**   **Dates of Birth**

Part II — Arrangements for the Children of the Family

3. Home Details *(Insert your current address here)*

    (a) The address or addresses at which the children now live.
        (Insert this information here.)

    (b) Give details of the number of living rooms, bedrooms etc. at the address in (a) above
        EXAMPLE: 3 bedrooms, 1 kitchen, 1 sittingroom and 1 bathroom

    (c) Is the house rented or owned and, if so, name tenant(s) or owner(s).
        EXAMPLE: Owner of house — . . . . This house is subject to a tenancy agreement with . . . . County Council.

    (d) Is the rent or mortgage being regularly paid and, if so, by whom?
        EXAMPLE: Mortgage is paid on a weekly basis by . . . . , Applicant.

    (e) Give the names of all other persons living with the children either on a full-time or part-time basis and state their relationship to the children, if any.
        (Insert names and relationships here, eg grandparent, child-minder etc.)

    (f) Will there be any change in these arrangements and, if so, give details.
        (Simply write No if the arrangements will remain the same. If any aspect of the children's living arrangements is going to change in the fore-seeable future for any reason, provide clear details.)

Part III — Education and Training Details

(a) Give the names of the school, college or place of training attended by each child. *(Insert schools' names and addresses.)*

(b) Do the children have any special educational needs? If so, please specify. *(Simply write No if the children have no special educational needs. If, however, a child is receiving — for example — special care or instruction for a learning disability, give specific details: type of disability, type of special instruction, where, how often.)*

(c) Is the school, college or place of training fee-paying? If so, give details of how much the fees are per term/year. Are fees being paid regularly and, if so, by whom? *(Simply write No is the school is not fee-paying. Otherwise, give specific details of how much these fees are, when they are paid, and by whom the fees are paid.)*

(d) Will there be any changes in these circumstances? If so, give details. *(Write No if the education arrangements will remain the same. Otherwise, give details: eg Child A is now at National School but will be attending . . . . , a fee-paying Secondary School, in September 20xx. School fees will amount to €. . . . , payable every . . . . by . . . . .)*

Part IV — Child-care Details

(a) Which parent looks after the children from day to day? If responsibility is shared, please give details. *EXAMPLE: Mother/Applicant.*

(b) Give details of work commitments of both parents. *EXAMPLE: Mother/Applicant — Part-time.* *Father/Respondent — Full-time.*

(c) Does someone look after the children when the parent is not there? If yes, give details. *(Insert details.)*

(d) Who looks after the children during the school holidays? *(Insert details.)*

(e) Will there be any changes in these circumstances? If yes, give details. *(Give details of any changes which are likely to occur in the answers given in a–d above.)*

Part V — Maintenance

(a) Does the Respondent pay towards the upkeep of the children? If yes, give details. Please specify any other source of maintenance.
(Provide details of how much the Respondent contributes to the upkeep of the children. If there are any other sources which provide maintenance, include them here.)

(b) Is the maintenance referred to at (a) above paid under court order? If yes, give details.
(Provide details.)

(c) Has maintenance for the children been agreed? If yes, give details.
(Some couples may have already agreed on a system for child maintenance, either between themselves or through mediation. Give specific details here. If no such agreement has been made, write No.)

(d) If not, will you be applying for a maintenance order from the Court?
(Specify your intentions here.)

Part VI — Details of Contact with the Children

(a) Do the children see the Applicant/Respondent? Please give details.
(Outline how/when both parents see the children.)

(b) Do the children stay overnight and/or have holiday visits with the Respondent/Applicant? Please give details.
EXAMPLE: Respondent/Applicant has unlimited access.

(c) Will there be any changes to these arrangements? Please give details.
(Describe whether contact arrangements are likely to change in any way. If not, write No.)

Part VII — Details of Health

(a) Are the children generally in good health? Please give details of any serious disability or chronic illness suffered by any of the children.
(Provide detailed information, including the name and age of any child to whom this applies. Otherwise, say that the children are in good health.)

(b) Do the children have any special health needs? Please give details of the care needed and how it is to be provided.
(Provide details.)

(c)   Are the Applicant and Respondent generally in good health? If not, please giv
      details.
      EXAMPLE: Applicant — Good Health.
      Respondent — Good Health.

Part VIII — Details of Care and Other Court Proceedings

(a)   Are the children or any of them in the care of a health board or under the super
      vision of a social worker or probation officer? If so, please specify.
      (Provide information.)

(b)   Are there or have there been any proceedings in any Court involving the childre
      or any of them? If so, please specify. (All relevant Court Orders relating to th
      children or any of them should be annexed hereto.)
      (Provide information as specified. Attach copies of any relevant documents.)

Part IX — Declaration

I, *(Insert your name)*, Applicant, declare that the information I have given herein i
correct and complete to the best of my knowledge.

Signed: _____

Witnessed: _____

Date: _____

Part X — Agreement of Respondent where Applicable

I, *(Insert Respondent's name)*, Respondent, declare that the information given by th
Applicant herein is correct and complete to the best of my knowledge and I agre
with the arrangements and proposals contained herein.

Signed: _____

Date: _____

AFFIDAVIT OF SERVICE

This document is proof that you (the Applicant) have served the *Family Law Civil Bill* on the Respondent. This is also one of the documents which must be sworn by a solicitor, which is done after the Family Law Civil Bill has been served. This document does not need a cover page.

When the *Family Law Civil Bill* has been served on the Respondent, this document is recorded proof of the date on which it was sent. If sent by registered post, the receipt of posting must be attached to your own copy of the *Affidavit of Service*.

AN CHUIRT TEAGHLAIGH CHUARDA
(THE CIRCUIT FAMILY COURT)

(Insert Circuit Court Name) **CIRCUIT** **COUNTY OF** *(Insert county name)*

IN THE MATTER OF THE FAMILY LAW (DIVORCE) ACT, 1996

BETWEEN *(Insert name of person applying for divorce)*
Applicant
AND
(Insert name of spouse, the person who is responding)
Respondent

AFFIDAVIT OF SERVICE

I, *(Insert your name, address and occupation here)*, aged 18 years and upwards MAKE OATH and say as follows:

1. That I did serve on the Respondent *(Insert name and address of Respondent here)* a true copy of The Family Law Civil Bill dated *(Insert date here)* by Personal Service/Registered Post. *[delete as necessary]*

2. I make this Affidavit from facts within my own knowledge save where otherwise appear and whereso appearing I believe the same to be true.

(Steps 1 and 2 already shown apply when giving the Family Law Civil Bill by hand. The following steps are to be inserted when sending by registered post.)

3. I bef to refer to certificate of posting of the said envelope attached hereto and signed by me prior to the swearing hereof.

4. I say that the envelope has not been returned undelivered.

SWORN By

This *(day)* day of *(month)* 20**xx**
Before me, a practising Solicitor, and
I know the Deponent/Declarant

_____ _____

Deponent/Declarant **Practising Solicitor**

NOTICE OF MOTION

When seeking a date for a hearing, the Applicant must bring this document to the local courthouse and present it to the court officials.

In preparing this document, leave blank spaces so the Clerk of the Court can insert the date, time and place of the court hearing.

Three copies of this document are needed. The court keeps one, the Applicant keeps one and the third copy is given to the Respondent. It does not need a cover page.

AN CHUIRT TEAGHLAIGH CHUARDA
(THE CIRCUIT FAMILY COURT)

(Insert Circuit Court Name) **CIRCUIT   COUNTY OF** *(Insert county name)*

IN THE MATTER OF THE FAMILY LAW (DIVORCE) ACT, 1996

BETWEEN   *(Insert name of person applying for divorce)*
                                                      Applicant
                                                      AND
                             (Insert name of spouse, the person who is responding)
                                                      Respondent

NOTICE OF MOTION

TAKE NOTICE that on the _____ day of _____ 20____
at _____ o'clock in the _____ or on the next opportunity thereafter, the
Applicant will apply to the Circuit Family Court sitting at Court No._____
for the judgement on consent against the Respondent in the terms of the
endorsement of claim on the Family Law Civil Bill herein.

WHICH application will be grounded upon the pleadings already herein, the
affidavit of service of this Notice of Motion, the nature of the case and the reasons
to be offered.

_____
Applicant

To: The County Registrar   To: *(Insert Respondent's name here)*
    (Insert relevant address here)   *(Insert relevant address here)*

SERVICE OF MOTION

This document is proof that the Applicant has served the *Notice of Motion* on the Respondent. It must be sworn by a solicitor after the Notice of Motion has been served. It does not need a cover page.

This document is similar to the *Affidavit of Service* (see page 59). If it is sent by registered post, the receipt must be attached to the Applicant's copy.

**AN CHUIRT TEAGHLAIGH CHUARDA
(THE CIRCUIT FAMILY COURT)**

(Insert Circuit Court Name) **CIRCUIT** **COUNTY OF** *(Insert county name)*

**IN THE MATTER OF THE FAMILY LAW
(DIVORCE) ACT, 1996**

BETWEEN *(Insert name of person applying for divorce)*
Applicant

AND

(Insert name of spouse, the person who is responding)
Respondent

SERVICE OF MOTION

, *(Insert name, address and occupation here)*, aged 18 years and upwards MAKE
OATH and say as follows:

.   That I did serve on the Respondent of *(insert address here)* a true copy of
    Notice of Motion dated the *(date)* day of *(month)* 20xx, by Personal
    Service/Registered Post. *(delete as appropriate)*.

2. I make this Affidavit from facts within my own knowledge save where
    otherwise appear and whereso appearing I believe the same to be true.

SWORN By

This   day of   20xx

Before me a practising Solicitor and I
know the Deponent/Declarant

_____   _____

Deponent/Declarant   **Practising Solicitor**

FINAL DIVORCE PAPERS

Following the successful completion of all documents and a positive hearing, the couple will be granted a Decree of Dissolution of Marriage.

Although details will differ, this decree will look like the following document. The final document will be signed, witnessed and stamped.

On the top of the page you will receive instructions to type four copies of this document.

RECORD NO. _____

AN CHUIRT TEAGHLAIGH CHUARDA
(THE CIRCUIT FAMILY COURT)

_____ CIRCUIT   COUNTY OF _____

BEFORE JUDGE _____

IN THE MATTER OF THE FAMILY LAW (DIVORCE) ACT, 1996

BETWEEN
(Insert name of person applying for divorce)
Applicant
AND
(Insert name of spouse, the person who is responding)
Respondent

The Family Law Civil Bill herein coming on for hearing before this Court this day on Notice of Motion dated _____ on behalf of the Applicant for Judgement by consent, as per the terms claimed in the Indorsement of Claim on the Family Law Civil Bill.

WHEREUPON AND ON READING the pleadings and documents filed herein and on hearing the evidence adduced and what was offered by the Applicant in person and the Respondent in person.

The Court Doth grant a Decree of Dissolution of the Marriage Solemnized on the _____, at the _____ in the County of _____ , between the said Applicant and Respondent, pursuant to the provisions of Section 5 (1) of the Family Law (Divorce) Act 1996.

And by consent it is further ordered pursuant to Section 18 (10) of the Family Law (Divorce) Act 1996 that the Applicant and Respndent shall not on the death of the other party, be entitled to apply for provision out of the other party's estate.

And the Court Doth make no order as to costs.

By the Court

EX PARTE DOCUMENTS

If your spouse (Respondent) is living outisde the State, the *Ex Parte Document* must be completed. It is then presented to the judge or County Registrar who must give permission for the Family Civil Law Bill and other relevant documents to be sent out of the country.

The following documents are examples of both the Applicant's document and the document which is completed by the Court.

(Sample of Applicant's Ex Parte Document)

Record No: 000/00

AN CHUIRT TEAGHLAIGH CHUARDA
(THE CIRCUIT FAMILY COURT)

(Insert Circuit Court Name) **CIRCUIT**   **COUNTY OF** *(Insert county name)*

IN THE MATTER OF THE FAMILY LAW (DIVORCE) ACT, 1996

BETWEEN   *(Insert name of person applying for divorce)*
                                                          Applicant
                                                          AND
                              (Insert name of spouse, the person who is responding)
                                                          Respondent

EX PARTE DOCUMENT

I desire to apply to the Court on the *(Insert date)* day of *(Month)*, 20xx in Court No. *(Insert court number and address of your local court)* at *(Insert time)* or the next opportunity thereafter for an order on behalf of the Applicant to the following effect:

To issue and serve the Family Law Civil Bill and all other documents outside of the State at: *(Insert foreign address here)*

The Application will be based on the oral evidence of the Applicant.

Dated the _____ day of _____ , 20xx.

                                              (Applicant's Name and Signature)

                                              _____
                                                          Applicant

To:
The County Registrar
(Insert local address)

(Sample of Ex Parte Documents from the Court)

RECORD No: 000/00

AN CHUIRT TEAGHLAIGH CHUARDA
(THE CIRCUIT FAMILY COURT)

(Insert Circuit Court Name) **CIRCUIT**   **COUNTY OF** *(Insert county name)*

BEFORE THE *(County Registrar or other Official)*

DATED THIS *(Insert date)*

IN THE MATTER OF THE FAMILY LAW (DIVORCE) ACT, 1996

BETWEEN   *(Insert name of person applying for divorce)*
Applicant
AND
(Insert name of spouse, the person who is responding)
Respondent

The Family Law Civil Bill herein coming on for hearing before me this day on ex parte on behalf of the Applicant for the relief as sought herein.

WHEREUPON AND ON READING the pleadings and documents filed herein and on hearing the evidencec tendered/adduced and what was offered by the Applicant in person.

I hereby order that the service of the Civil Bill in these proceedings be deemed good.

I further order service of the subsequent documents outside of the jurisdiction at *(Insert foreign address here)*

and certificate of posting to be exhibited in respect of such service.

Allow 28 days for the finding of a defence and reserve costs.

_____

County Registrar

CERTIFICATE OF NO APPEARANCE/DEFENCE

This will be used by the County Registrar when the Respondent fails to respond and has ignored the paperwork sent by the Applicant.

The Applicant brings this document into the court when lodging documents such as the *Affidavit of Service*. This *Certificate of No Appearance/Defence* is normally put on file until it is needed.

AN CHUIRT TEAGHLAIGH CHUARDA
(THE CIRCUIT FAMILY COURT)

(Insert Circuit Court Name) **CIRCUIT** **COUNTY OF** *(Insert county name)*

IN THE MATTER OF THE FAMILY LAW
(DIVORCE) ACT, 1996

BETWEEN *(Insert name of person applying for divorce)*
Applicant

AND

(Insert name of spouse, the person who is responding)
Respondent

CERTIFICATE OF NO APPEARANCE/DEFENCE

THIS IS to certify that no appearance/defence has been filed by the Respondent for the Family Law Civil Bill issued on *(Insert date on which this document was served).*

Signed By:

_____

County Registrar

NOTICE TO TRUSTEES

This applies only to people with pensions. Where applicable, copies of the following must be sent to the pension manager of the relevant company or companies.

The following documents are used when both parties are in agreement regarding the sharing of any pension scheme. They include:

- a *covering letter* from the Applicant
- a document entitled *Notice to Trustees*
- a further document entitled *Consent*, with the witnessed signatures of both the Applicant and Respondent

Where there is disagreement, the assistance of a solicitor is advisable.

(Sample of Notice to Trustees to be sent to Pensions Manager/s)

AN CHUIRT TEAGHLAIGH CHUARDA
(THE CIRCUIT FAMILY COURT)

(Insert Circuit Court Name) **CIRCUIT   COUNTY OF** *(Insert county name)*

IN THE MATTER OF THE FAMILY LAW (DIVORCE) ACT, 1996

BETWEEN   *(Insert name of person applying for divorce)*
                                                                    Applicant
                                                                         AND
                              (Insert name of spouse, the person who is responding)
                                                                  Respondent

NOTICE TO TRUSTEES

TAKE NOTICE that relief has been claimed by the Applicant in the above entitled proceedings pursuant to Section 17 of the Family Law (Divorce) Act 1996 and in particular in relation to *(Insert name of Applicant)*, the Applicant herein, and her/his pension with *(Insert name of pension company here)*.

AND TAKE FURTHER NOTICE that the Notice of Trial to fix a date for Trial will be served upon you in due course in accordance with the rules of the Circuit Court.

Dated the _____ day of _____ 20xx

Signed: _____
(Typed name of Applicant)
Applicant

To:
  *(Insert Name of Company
  Name of Pensions Manager Address)*

(Sample of Letter which accompanies Documents sent to Pensions Manager/s)

To:
    (Insert Name of Company
    Name of Pensions Manager
    Address)

Re: In the matter of the Family Law (Divorce) Act 1996

Between: *(Insert name of Applicant)*
    And
    (Insert name of Respondent)

I am the Applicant in the above-mentioned proceedings. As you are aware, I have a pension scheme with you. Accordingly, I serve upon you a "Notice of Trustees' with regard to the said pension.

I would point out that Trustees would be required to take <u>No steps</u>, as the only order being sought by me, the Applicant, from the Respondent is a nil order and subsequent blocking order in respect of each of my and the Respondent's pension scheme entitlements. I herewith enclose a copy of the applications which you will note have been executed by me and the Respondent.

Yours faithfully,

_____

(Typed name here)

(Sample of Consent to be sent to Pensions Manager/s)

AN CHUIRT TEAGHLAIGH CHUARDA
(THE CIRCUIT FAMILY COURT)

(Insert Circuit Court Name) **CIRCUIT   COUNTY OF** *(Insert county name)*

IN THE MATTER OF THE FAMILY LAW (DIVORCE) ACT, 1996

BETWEEN   *(Insert name of person applying for divorce)*
Applicant
AND
(Insert name of spouse, the person who is responding)
Respondent

CONSENT

TAKE NOTICE that we _____ , Applicant, and _____, Respondent, consent to the granting of the following orders pursuant to the Family Law (Divorce) Act 1996.

1. An order pursuant to the provisions of Section 5 (1) of the said Act for a Decree of Divorce from the Respondent to the Applicant herein in terms of the existing Consent Orders made by his/her Honour Judge _____ dated the _____ day of 20xx and made before Judge _____ dated the _____ day of _____ 20xx in the matter of the Judicial Separation and Family Law Reform Act 1989 and in the matter of the Family Law Act 1995, together with:

   (a) An order pursuant to Section 18 (10) of the said Act that the Respondent herein shall not on the death of the Applicant, be entitled to apply for an order under Section 18 of the said Act.

   (b) A nil pension adjustment order pursuant to Section 17 of the 1996 Act, together with a preclusion on any further variations of said nil order pursuant to Section 17 (26) of the 1996 Act.

   (c) Such further or no orders as his Honourable Court shall deem meet and just.

$\rightarrow$

CONSENT (cont.)

(d) Each party to be responsible for his or her own costs in these proceedings.

IN WITNESS HEREOF THE PARTIES HERETO HAVE HEREUNDER SET THEIR HANDS AND AFFIXED THEIR SEALS THIS _____ DAY OF 20xx.

SIGNED, SEALED AND DELIVERED BY THE SAID APPLICANT _____ IN THE PRESENCE OF _____ .

SIGNED, SEALED AND DELIVERED BY THE SAID RESPONDENT _____ IN THE PRESENCE OF _____ .

NON-AMICABLE DIVORCE

By law, a couple is entitled to seek a divorce if they have been living apart for four consecutive years out of the last five.

However, even where this situation exists, a spouse (the Respondent) may continue to contest the divorce for various reasons. In this case, a person can still represent him/herself in the divorce proceedings, even if the Respondent is represented by a solicitor. All the rules and instructions given here still apply.

If you yourself are contesting a divorce, you have 20 days from the date of receiving the *Family Law Civil Bill* to deliver a statement in writing to the court showing the nature and grounds of your defence.

Seeking Mediation

In cases in which the divorce is obviously not going to be amicable, the couple may choose to seek mediation. The Family Mediation Service run by the Department of Social, Community and Family Affairs is a free, professional and confidential service for couples who have decided to separate or divorce and who wish to negotiate the terms of their separation or divorce with the help of a trained mediator. The service assists divorcing or separating couples to look at the resources and options open to them and to reach an agreement which meets the interests of both parties and the interests of the children.

When a couple arrives at a Family Mediation Centre, they are first seen together by their mediator. The mediator, who is neither a counsellor nor a legal adviser, will emphasise that the couple themselves will be the decision-makers in this process. It is not the mediator's role to make decisions but to facilitate the discussions and manage the couple's negotiations.

At this intitial session, the mediator will ask why the couple has opted for mediation, what their expectations for mediation are, and what issues they need to discuss in order to reach agreement.

The couple then create their own agenda of issues for negotiation.

Issues for Mediation

When a couple in dispute over a divorce go for mediation, the issues for mediation frequently include:

- The Family Home — Where will each person live? Where will the children live?

- Parenting — How will the children spend time with each of their parents? How will the parents communicate about their children?

- Financial Support — Will support be paid for one spouse and the children? How much will each person have to live on?

- Pensions — What entitlements are there? How will they be distributed?

- Assets — How will the couple divide their assets?

- Debts — How will the couple manage their debts and other out-goings?

- Contents of the Family Home — How will the contents be distributed?

Having set their agenda, the parties provide information on their future financial requirements which are set out on a budget sheet which includes information on both parties' incomes. Where property is involved, it may be necessary to obtain a valuation on the property, as well as the value and benefits of any pension scheme.

If the couple has not sought legal advice and one or the other decides that they intend to use a solicitor to contest their divorce, they may need to seek that advice in the course of mediation. Mediation's principle is that information is power: the better informed the couple is, the better the decisions they will make.

Note of Mediated Agreement

When the couple has reached agreement on all the issues on their agenda, the mediator draws up a *Note of Mediated Agreement* in easy-to-understand language. The parties can then take the *Note of Mediated Agreement* to their respective solicitors who will draw up a Separation Agreement based on the mediation. This agreement is important background information if disagreements continue to arise in divorce proceedings.

Useful Information and Addresses

The Family Mediation Service produces literature which helps families understand the impact of separation and divorce on their lives. Their Information Pack deals with the following issues:

- What is a parenting plan?

- Managing the stress of separation and divorce

- The end of a marriage — a time of grieving and loss

- How children react to separation or divorce

- We are separating — what do we tell the children?

- Managing the financial issues at separation or divorce

Dublin Area

The Family Mediation Services can be contacted at the following three Dublin addresses.
Family Mediation Service
1st Floor
St Stephen's Green House
Earlsfort Terrace
Dublin 2
Phone: (01) 634 4320
Fax: (01) 662 2339

Family Mediation Service
c/o Accord Office
71 Griffith Avenue
Marino
Dublin 3
Phone: (01) 818 6050
Fax: (01) 833 8679

Family Mediation Service
The Rere
Tallaght Social Service Centre
The Square
Dublin 24
Phone: (01) 414 5180
Fax: (01) 462 5956

Full-time offices outside Dublin

Hibernian House
80a South Mall
Cork
Phone: (021) 252 200
Fax: (021) 251 331

1st Floor
Ross House
Merchant's Road
Galway
Phone: (091) 509 730
Fax: (091) 567 623

1st Floor
Mill House
Henry Street
Limerick
Phone: (061) 214 310
Fax: (061) 312 2225

Part-time offices

Kerry Family Resource and Counselling
    Centre
Balloonagh
Tralee
Co. Kerry
Phone: (066) 718 6100
Fax: (066) 712 9332

3 Seatown Place
Dundalk
Co. Louth
Phone: (042) 935 9410
Fax: (042) 933 8514

Family Centre Castlebar
Chapel St
Castlebar
Co. Mayo
Phone: (091) 509730
Fax: (091) 567623

CIC
St Mary's Square
Athlone
Co. Westmeath
Phone: (0902) 20970
Fax: (0902) 77011

Distillery Road
Wexford
Phone: (053) 63050
Fax: (053) 23576

STATISTICS

There has been a steady increase in the divorce rate since it was first introduced in Ireland in 1997.

While Ireland cannot compare itself to Britain where the divorce rate is the highest in Europe (two-out-of-five marriages there end in divorce), the charts on pages 95–97 nevertheless indicate that Irish divorce statistics are alarming.

When divorce was first legalised in Ireland, applications were slow. By the end of the first year, 431 applications had been received by the Courts Service, though only 95 divorces were granted that year. The figure for the same period in the following year (1998) had jumped to 2,761 applications, of which 1,421 were granted.

In the year ending 31 December 2000, the numbers seeking divorce had again increased significantly, with 2,740 applications granted out of 3,380 received.

Predictably, the largest number of divorces sought (1,536) and granted (1,170) in the millennium year were in Dublin. The other two cities where the highest number of divorces occurred were Cork — where 373 divorces were sought in the year 2000 (280 granted) — and Limerick — where 119 divorces were sought and 94 were granted.

Provincial towns also saw an increase in the number of divorces applied for and granted. In Dundalk, for instance, 85 divorces were sought and 71 granted. In Wicklow town, 135 divorces were sought and 98 granted in 2000, while the figures for Wexford were 98 applications and 76 granted.

The latest statistics, those for 2001, show a further slight increase in the divorce rate. In that year, there were 3,459 divorce applications (compared to 3,339 for 2000). Of these 2,817 divorces were granted (compared with 2,710 in the millenium year).

The statistics shown on pages 95–97 give a breakdown of the numbers of divorces sought and granted since divorce was introduced in Ireland. The figures also show the number of judicial separations sought and granted, and the number of nullity applications sought and granted over those years. Further statistics show precisely where divorces, judicial separations and nullity applications were sought and granted in 2001.

DIVORCE, JUDICIAL SEPARATION AND NULLITY APPLICATIONS RECEIVED AND DEALT WITH IN ALL JURISDICTIONS 1995 TO 2001

Year ending 31st July 1995

	Judicial Separation Applications		Divorce Applications		Nullity Applications	
	Received	Granted	Received	Granted	Received	Granted
Circuit Courts	1,398	929				
High Court	48	21			66	31
Supreme Court	3	1			1	1
TOTAL	**1,449**	**951**			**67**	**32**

Year ending 31st July 1996

	Judicial Separation Applications		Divorce Applications		Nullity Applications	
	Received	Granted	Received	Granted	Received	Granted
Circuit Courts	1,670	1,185				
High Court	69	28			84	46
Supreme Court	1	2			2	1
TOTAL	**1,740**	**1,215**			**86**	**47**

Year ending 31st July 1997

	Judicial Separation Applications		Divorce Applications		Nullity Applications	
	Received	Granted	Received	Granted	Received	Granted
Circuit Courts	1,208	1,431	423	93	28	3
High Court	54	50	8	2	20	50
Supreme Court	1	0	0	0	0	0
TOTAL	**1,263**	**1,481**	**431**	**95**	**48**	**53**

Year ending 31st July 1998

	Judicial Separation Applications		Divorce Applications		Nullity Applications	
	Received	Granted	Received	Granted	Received	Granted
Circuit Courts	1,525	920	2,725	1,408	63	23
High Court	56	26	36	13	12	47
Supreme Court	5					
TOTAL	**1,586**	**946**	**2,761**	**1,421**	**5**	**70**

Year ending 31st July 1999

	Judicial Separation Applications		Divorce Applications		Nullity Applications	
	Received	Granted	Received	Granted	Received	Granted
Circuit Courts	1,536	967	3,293	2,315	86	34
High Court	59	32	23	18	5	20
Supreme Court	2					
TOTAL	**1,597**	**999**	**3,316**	**2,333**	**91**	**54**

Year ending 31st July 2000

	Judicial Separation Applications		Divorce Applications		Nullity Applications	
	Received	Granted	Received	Granted	Received	Granted
Circuit Courts	1,554	995	3,311	2,596	90	51
High Court	67	40	35	27	8	5
Supreme Court	3	3	3	1		
TOTAL	**1,624**	**1,038**	**3,349**	**2,624**	**98**	**56**

Year ending 31st December 2000

	Judicial Separation Applications		Divorce Applications		Nullity Applications	
	Received	Granted	Received	Granted	Received	Granted
Circuit Courts	1,592	998	3,339	2,710	84	47
High Court	76	27	39	30	8	5
Supreme Court*	5		2			
TOTAL	**1,673**	**1,025**	**3,380**	**2,740**	**92**	**52**

*1/8/00 to 31/12/00

Year ending 31st December 2001

	Judicial Separation Applications		Divorce Applications		Nullity Applications	
	Received	Granted	Received	Granted	Received	Granted
Circuit Courts	1,845	1,018	3,459	2,817	109	59
High Court	76	27	31	20	8	4
Supreme Court	2		3	1		
TOTAL	**1,923**	**1,045**	**3,493**	**2,838**	**117**	**63**

TOTAL APPLICATIONS RECEIVED AND DEALT WITH IN ALL JURISDICTIONS

Year ending	Judicial Separation Applications		Divorce Applications		Nullity Applications	
	Received	Granted	Received	Granted	Received	Granted
31st July 1995	1,449	951			67	32
31st July 1996	1,740	1,215			86	47
31st July 1997	1,263	1,481	431	95	48	53
31st July 1998	1,586	946	2,761	1,421	75	70
31st July 1999	1,597	999	3,316	2,333	91	54
31st July 2000	1,624	1,038	3,349	2,624	98	56
31st December 2000	1,673	1,025	3,380	2,740	92	52
31st December 2001	1,923	1,045	3,493	2,838	117	63

DIVORCE, JUDICIAL SEPARATION AND NULLITY APPLICATIONS RECEIVED AND GRANTED BY THE CIRCUIT COURTS IN YEAR ENDING 31/12/01.

	DIVORCE APPLICATIONS				JUDICIAL SEPARATIONS			
	Received	Granted	Refused	wd/so	Received	Granted	Refused	wd/so
CARLOW	46	41	0	2	30	17	0	1
CARRICK ON SHANNON	8	9	0	0	9	6	0	
CASTLEBAR	52	49	0	0	48	30	0	0
CAVAN	21	30	0	0	20	23	0	0
CLONMEL	83	66	0	2	46	19	0	0
CORK	397	340	0	0	244	199	0	10
DUBLIN	1,398	1,096	0	0	678	249	1	1
DUNDALK	87	67	0	0	65	36	0	0
ENNIS	81	79	0	1	29	35	0	0
GALWAY	115	111	0	4	50	48	0	2
KILKENNY	49	39	0	2	32	23	0	8
LETTERKENNY	74	80	0	3	44	37	0	1
LIMERICK	148	147	0	2	69	34	0	2
LONGFORD	23	15	0	2	11	5	0	1
MONAGHAN	37	12	0	0	30	21	0	1
MULLINGAR	68	47	1	1	21	17	0	1
NAAS	136	73	0	0	74	21	0	1
PORTLAOISE	31	30	0	0	23	19	0	1
ROSCOMMON	45	31	0	0	40	16	0	1
SLIGO	36	37	0	1	28	23	0	1
TRALEE	75	43	0	0	56	24	0	1
TRIM	76	56	0	0	53	34	0	0
TULLAMORE	44	27	0	3	20	13	0	2
WATERFORD	122	101	0	6	42	35	0	3
WEXFORD	100	83	0	18	29	14	0	11
WICKLOW	107	108	0	0	54	20	0	3
TOTAL	3,459	2,817	1	47	1,845	1,018	1	52

$\longrightarrow$

**DIVORCE, JUDICIAL SEPARATION AND NULLITY APPLICATIONS RECEIVED
AND GRANTED BY THE CIRCUIT COURTS IN YEAR ENDING 31/12/01. (cont.)**

	NULLITY APPLICATIONS				SECTION 33			APPEALS	
Received	Granted	Refused	wd/so	Received	Granted	Refused	Received	Dealt with
0	0	0	0	48	43	0	5	6
0	0	0	0	10	10	0	2	1
2	2	0	0	17	17	0	5	2
1	2	0	0	21	19	0	1	0
1	1	0	0	22	22	0	14	12
20	24	0	0	73	73	0	39	26
68	9	0	0	466	455	11	251	125
0	2	0	0	0	0	0	28	27
1	2	0	0	20	19	1	8	4
5	5	0	0	63	60	3	17	17
0	2	0	0	33	30	0	4	3
2	3	0	0	54	54	0	2	6
1	1	0	0	44	42	2	16	12
0	0	0	0	12	12	0	7	5
0	0	0	0	22	22	0	2	4
1	1	0	0	14	13	1	5	6
3	2	0	1	50	50	0	16	18
1	0	0	1	27	27	0	8	6
0	0	1	0	13	13	0	4	6
0	0	0	0	16	16	0	1	0
0	0	0	0	31	29	2	25	26
1	2	0	0	40	27	4	15	4
0	0	0	0	40	38	1	2	2
0	0	0	0	30	30	0	0	0
0	0	0	0	23	23	0	0	7
2	1	0	0	21	16	4	6	6
109	59	1	2	1,210	1,160	29	483	331

DIVORCE, JUDICIAL SEPARATION AND NULLITY APPLICATIONS RECEIVED AND GRANTED BY THE CIRCUIT COURTS IN YEAR ENDING 31/07/00.

	DIVORCE APPLICATIONS				JUDICIAL SEPARATIONS				NULLITY APPLICATIONS			
	Received	Granted	Refused	wd/so	Received	Granted	Refused	wd/so	Received	Granted	Refused	wd/so
CARLOW	54	41	0	0	11	4	0	0	2	2	0	0
CARRICK ON SHANNON	13	8	0	0	11	7	0	2	0	0	0	0
CASTLEBAR	62	50	0	0	48	18	0	1	2	4	0	0
CAVAN	28	15	0	1	10	13	0	0	1	1	0	0
CLONMEL *	90	63	0	1	34	24	0	3	1	1	0	0
CORK	373	280	0	0	258	121	0	0	13	15	0	0
DUBLIN	1,536	1,170	0	57	517	367	0	12	47	15	1	3
DUNDALK	85	71	0	0	31	39	0	0	3	0	0	0
ENNIS	59	57	0	0	49	31	0	1	2	1	0	0
GALWAY	79	37	0	0	58	34	0	0	3	0	1	0
KILKENNY	40	49	0	1	27	9	0	1	0	0	0	0
LETTERKENNY #	49	42	0	0	31	15	0	0	2	0	0	0
LIMERICK	119	94	0	7	52	35	0	0	1	1	0	0
LONGFORD	11	14	0	0	10	4	0	0	0	0	0	0
MONAGHAN	15	22	0	1	26	26	0	2	0	1	0	0
MULLINGAR	49	51	0	0	30	19	0	1	2	1	0	0
NAAS	110	60	0	2	63	43	0	3	2	2	0	0
PORTLAOISE	33	25	0	0	10	4	0	1	1	1	0	0
ROSCOMMON	18	16	0	0	17	11	0	1	2	1	0	0
SLIGO	46	39	0	2	33	21	0	1	0	0	0	0
TRALEE	41	46	1	1	46	33	0	3	1	1	0	0
TRIM	50	72	0	2	41	30	0	6	2	1	0	0
TULLAMORE	32	33	0	0	15	14	0	2	0	0	0	0
WATERFORD	86	67	0	1	36	26	0	1	1	0	0	0
WEXFORD	98	76	0	58	41	21	0	35	1	1	0	1
WICKLOW	135	98	0	1	49	26	0	3	1	3	0	0
TOTAL C.C.	3,311	2,596	1	135	1,554	995	0	78	90	51	2	4

NOTE: Category WD/SO also includes applications which were adjourned generally with liberty to re-enter.
*1 divorce granted on foot of nullity application. # 2 judicial separation applications amended to divorce applications.

DIVORCE, JUDICIAL SEPARATION AND NULLITY APPLICATIONS RECEIVED AND GRANTED BY THE CIRCUIT COURTS IN YEAR ENDING 31/12/00.

	DIVORCE APPLICATIONS				JUDICIAL SEPARATIONS				NULLITY APPLICATIONS			
	Received	Granted	Refused	wd/so	Received	Granted	Refused	wd/so	Received	Granted	Refused	wd/so
CARLOW	47	58	0	0	14	5	0	0	1	1	0	0
CARRICK ON SHANNON	15	5	0	0	9	6	0	0	1	0	0	0
CASTLEBAR	60	45	0	0	49	27	0	3	1	3	0	0
CAVAN	27	15	0	0	12	10	0	0	2	0	0	0
CLONMEL	90	80	0	1	34	25	0	2	0	1	0	0
CORK	384	307	0	0	264	129	0	0	15	14	0	0
DUBLIN	1,395	1,126	3	57	527	347	0	14	40	14	1	2
DUNDALK	103	92	0	0	29	31	0	1	3	0	0	0
ENNIS	70	59	0	0	45	30	0	1	1	0	0	0
GALWAY	63	63	0	0	34	28	0	0	5	1	1	0
KILKENNY	54	36	0	0	27	9	0	0	0	0	0	0
LETTERKENNY	69	44	0	2	38	17	0	2	2	1	0	0
LIMERICK	171	123	0	8	52	39	0	0	0	0	0	0
LONGFORD	14	10	0	0	7	7	0	0	0	1	0	0
MONAGHAN	18	19	0	0	17	25	0	0	1	1	0	0
MULLINGAR	55	52	0	3	25	17	0	2	1	2	0	0
NAAS	128	94	0	2	78	57	0	6	4	2	0	0
PORTLAOISE	37	34	0	0	16	3	0	0	0	0	0	0
ROSCOMMON	32	14	0	0	28	13	0	0	0	1	0	0
SLIGO	45	33	0	0	29	20	0	1	1	0	0	0
TRALEE	44	44	1	0	40	32	0	3	1	1	0	0
TRIM	60	64	0	2	56	29	0	7	3	2	0	0
TULLAMORE	37	28	0	1	31	14	0	2	0	0	0	0
WATERFORD	89	71	0	0	40	24	0	0	1	0	0	0
WEXFORD	92	85	0	26	40	26	0	32	1	1	0	2
WICKLOW	140	109	0	0	51	28	0	0	2	2	0	0
TOTAL	3,339	2,710	4	102	1,592	998	0	76	84	47	2	4

NOTE: Category WD/SO also includes applications which were adjourned generally with liberty to re-enter.

DIVORCE, JUDICIAL SEPARATION AND NULLITY APPLICATIONS RECEIVED AND GRANTED BY THE CIRCUIT COURTS IN YEAR ENDING 31/07/99.

	DIVORCE APPLICATIONS				JUDICIAL SEPARATIONS				NULLITY APPLICATIONS			
	Received	Granted	Refused	wd/so	Received	Granted	Refused	wd/so	Received	Granted	Refused	wd/so
CARLOW	53	46	0	0	13	23	0	0	0	2	0	0
CARRICK ON SHANNON	8	10	0	0	15	9	0	1	1	1	0	0
CASTLEBAR	58	47	0	0	33	19	1	1	3	0	0	0
CAVAN	18	17	0	0	21	12	0	2	0	0	0	0
CLONMEL	48	32	0	1	38	14	0	1	0	0	0	0
CORK	313	207	0	0	237	116	0	0	25	9	1	0
DUBLIN	1,653	1,117	3	61	470	380	0	25	26	10	1	0
DUNDALK	101	43	1	1	72	17	0	0	5	4	1	0
ENNIS	68	54	0	0	38	18	0	0	5	2	0	0
GALWAY	73	52	0	0	83	66	0	1	2	2	0	0
KILKENNY	50	29	0	0	19	18	0	5	0	0	0	0
LETTERKENNY	34	42	0	0	28	26	0	1	1	1	0	0
LIMERICK	118	108	0	2	57	45	0	0	4	0	0	0
LONGFORD	24	15	0	0	8	6	0	0	0	0	0	0
MONAGHAN	20	15	0	0	34	20	0	2	1	0	0	0
MULLINGAR	56	40	0	0	26	11	0	1	2	0	0	0
NAAS	83	58	0	4	64	40	0	4	1	1	0	0
PORTLAOISE	19	6	0	1	8	3	0	0	0	0	0	0
ROSCOMMON	20	14	0	0	18	11	0	0	1	0	0	0
SLIGO	33	24	0	0	25	14	0	2	2	0	0	0
TRALEE	53	60	0	0	60	27	0	0	2	0	0	0
TRIM	74	48	0	0	31	17	0	0	2	0	0	0
TULLAMORE	36	20	0	0	27	6	0	0	2	0	0	0
WATERFORD	115	88	0	0	27	18	0	0	0	0	0	1
WEXFORD	75	71	0	0	40	24	0	1	1	0	0	0
WICKLOW	90	52	0	0	44	17	0	4	2	2	1	0
TOTAL	3,293	2,315	4	70	1,536	967	1	51	86	34	3	1

DIVORCE, JUDICIAL SEPARATION AND NULLITY APPLICATIONS RECEIVED AND GRANTED BY THE CIRCUIT COURTS IN 1999.

	DIVORCE APPLICATIONS				JUDICIAL SEPARATIONS				NULLITY APPLICATIONS			
	Received	Granted	Refused	wd/so	Received	Granted	Refused	wd/so	Received	Granted	Refused	wd/so
CARLOW	53	33	0	0	10	6	0	0	1	1	0	0
CARRICK ON SHANNON	6	11	0	0	13	8	0	0	1	1	0	0
CASTLEBAR	60	44	0	0	37	14	0	1	4	2	0	0
CAVAN	19	18	0	1	16	14	0	1	0	0	0	0
CLONMEL	59	27	0	1	37	22	0	3	1	0	0	0
CORK	328	222	0	0	230	125	0	0	19	10	0	0
DUBLIN	1,564	1,217	3	36	492	415	0	16	32	10	0	0
DUNDALK	97	49	1	1	64	20	0	0	5	1	0	2
ENNIS	74	53	0	0	46	26	0	0	4	2	1	0
GALWAY	67	67	0	0	74	70	0	4	4	2	1	0
KILKENNY	43	42	0	1	22	17	0	2	0	0	0	0
LETTERKENNY	42	56	0	0	25	40	0	0	0	0	0	0
LIMERICK	118	84	0	0	57	43	0	0	3	0	0	0
LONGFORD	17	19	0	0	11	5	0	0	0	0	0	0
MONAGHAN	21	15	0	0	36	20	0	0	0	0	0	0
MULLINGAR	45	47	0	0	30	11	0	1	0	0	0	0
NAAS	83	45	0	0	42	24	0	0	3	1	0	0
PORTLAOISE	18	8	0	0	8	2	0	0	1	1	0	0
ROSCOMMON	18	13	0	0	10	8	0	0	2	1	0	0
SLIGO	40	16	0	1	34	13	0	3	0	0	0	0
TRALEE	51	54	0	1	55	29	0	0	0	0	0	0
TRIM	63	52	0	1	30	18	0	0	0	0	0	0
TULLAMORE	36	25	0	0	35	5	0	0	1	0	0	0
WATERFORD	121	100	0	0	27	21	0	1	1	0	0	0
WEXFORD	93	54	0	1	38	19	0	1	2	0	0	1
WICKLOW	100	59	0	3	46	14	0	3	1	1	1	0
TOTAL	3,236	2,430	4	47	1,525	1,009	0	36	84	33	3	3

DIVORCE, JUDICIAL SEPARATION AND NULLITY APPLICATIONS RECEIVED AND GRANTED BY THE CIRCUIT COURTS IN YEAR ENDING 31/7/98

	DIVORCE APPLICATIONS		JUDICIAL SEPARATION APPLICATIONS		NULLITY APPLICATIONS	
	Received	Granted	Received	Granted	Received	Granted
CARLOW	34	9	19	2	0	0
CARRICK ON SHANNON	9	6	10	7	0	0
CASTLEBAR	62	27	49	17	4	3
CAVAN	26	12	16	9	0	0
CLONMEL	64	31	41	31	0	0
CORK	268	131	228	107	15	5
DUBLIN	1,277	715	567	421	24	9
DUNDALK	76	35	37	41	0	0
ENNIS	48	25	38	13	0	0
GALWAY	59	61	21	29	1	1
KILKENNY	45	18	37	20	0	0
LETTERKENNY	57	19	59	13	0	0
LIMERICK	105	34	68	33	1	1
LONGFORD	17	16	5	2	0	0
MONAGHAN	26	11	40	20	2	0
MULLINGAR	42	20	13	7	0	0
NAAS	67	28	47	17	0	0
PORTLAOISE	16	8	14	4	1	0
ROSCOMMON	11	10	8	7	1	1
SLIGO	18	15	12	5	0	0
TRALEE	89	31	44	28	0	0
TRIM	54	26	30	19	3	0
TULLAMORE	20	14	17	7	0	0
WATERFORD	72	21	24	9	1	1
WEXFORD	88	53	27	29	0	0
WICKLOW	75	32	54	23	10	2
TOTAL	2,725	1,408	1,525	920	63	23

DIVORCE, JUDICIAL SEPARATION AND NULLITY APPLICATIONS RECEIVED AND GRANTED BY THE CIRCUIT COURTS IN YEAR ENDING 31/7/97

	DIVORCE APPLICATIONS		JUDICIAL SEPARATION APPLICATIONS		NULLITY APPLICATIONS	
	Received	Granted	Received	Granted	Received	Granted
CARLOW	1	1	13	26		0
CARRICK ON SHANNON	1	1	15	11		0
CASTLEBAR	2	3	30	25		1
CAVAN	5	1	16	10		0
CLONMEL	5	0	36	54		0
CORK	44	4	172	124	5	1
DUBLIN	216	49	448	659	14	1
DUNDALK	5	3	50	42	3	0
ENNIS	12	4	23	37	1	0
GALWAY	14	7	23	65		0
KILKENNY	3	0	14	19		0
LETTERKENNY	3	2	22	15		0
LIMERICK	10	0	32	60	1	0
LONGFORD	0	0	5	6		0
MONAGHAN	0	0	31	21		0
MULLINGAR	4	2	20	19		0
NAAS	18	1	50	28		0
PORTLAOISE	4	1	25	14	1	0
ROSCOMMON	3	0	16	11		0
SLIGO	6	6	8	11		0
TRALEE	9	1	25	12		0
TRIM	12	1	33	30	2	0
TULLAMORE	4	1	9	18		0
WATERFORD	20	0	14	22		0
WEXFORD	8	2	34	32	1	0
WICKLOW	14	3	44	60		0
TOTAL	423	93	1,208	1,431	28	3

GLOSSARY

AFFIDAVIT A written declaration made under oath before a notary public or other authorised officer.

APPLICANT The one who initiates divorce proceedings and applies for a divorce.

DECLARANT Someone who make a formal, often legal, statement.

DEPONENT Someone who makes an affidavit or who testifies under oath.

EX-PARTE From or on one side only. Said of a court application.

OATH A formal statement declaring the truth of a claim or promising to fulfil a pledge.

JUDICAL SEPARATION A court order recognising that husband and wife are living apart and regulating their mutual rights and liabilities. Also refereed to as a legal separation.

NOTICE OF MOTION A motion where notice is given to the other side in legal proceedings. Unless the High Court gives special leave to the contrary, there must be at least two clear days between the service of a Notice of Motion for the hearing of the motion. However, where the notice of motion requires to be served personally out of court, it must be served not less than four clear days before the hearing of the application.

RELIEF In this instance it refers to each person letting go of the pensions.

RESPONDENT A person who responds to the divorce proceedings.

SCHEDULE A written list or statement, usually in tabular form. A supplementary statement of details appended to a document.

SERVICE OF MOTION A legal document which the applicant fills in when the respondent is served with the Notice of Motion. This document in automatically follows a Notice of Motion in a divorce.

TRUSTEE A person or agent holding legal title to property in order to administer it for a beneficiary.